SCIENTIFIC AMERICAN® EDUCATIONAL PUBLISHING

SCIENCE IN ACTION

10 FUN
PHYSICS PROJECTS

T0182687

BRING SCIENCE HOME

Published in 2025 by The Rosen Publishing Group, Inc.
2544 Clinton Street, Buffalo, NY 14224

Contains material from Scientific American , a division of Springer Nature America, Inc., reprinted by permission as well as original material from The Rosen Publishing Group.

Editor: Kristen Rajczak Nelson
Designer: Rachel Rising

Activity on p. 5 by Science Buddies, Sabine De Brabandere (March 5, 2020); p. 9 by Science Buddies, Svenja Lohner (June 13, 2019); p.15 by Science Buddies, Sabine De Brabandere (April 4, \2019); p. 19 by Science Buddies, Ben Finio (February 25, 2016); p. 25 by Science Buddies (January 28, 2016); p. 31 by Science Buddies (June 26, 2014); p. 37 by Science Buddies, Sabine De Brabandere (November 23, 2017); p. 43 by Science Buddies, Ben Finio (August 11, 2016); p. 49 by Science Buddies, Svenja Lohner (April 12, 2018); p. 55 by Science Buddies, Megan Arnett (August 31, 2017).

All illustrations by Continuum Content Solutions

Photo Credits: pp. 2, 3, 15, 18, 25, 29, 31, 34, 49, 52 cve iv/Shutterstock.com; pp. 5, 19, 15, 19, 25, 31, 37, 43, 49, 55 Anna Frajtova/Shutterstock.com.

Cataloging-in-Publication Data

Names: Scientific American, Inc.
Title: Science in action: 10 fun physics projects / edited by the Scientific American Editors.
Description: New York : Scientific American Educational Publishing, an imprint of Rosen Publishing, 2025. | Series: Bring science home | Includes glossary and index.
Identifiers: ISBN 9781725350632 (pbk.) | ISBN 9781725350649 (library bound) | ISBN 9781725350656 (ebook)
Subjects: LCSH: Physics--Experiments--Juvenile literature. | Physics--Juvenile literature.
Classification: LCC QC25.S39 2025 | DDC 530.078--dc23

Manufactured in the United States of America

Some of the images in this book illustrate individuals who are models. The depictions do not imply actual situations or events.

CPSIA Compliance Information: Batch #CSSA25. For further information contact Rosen Publishing, New York, New York at 1-800-237-9932.

Find us on

CONTENTS

⊛ THESE ACTIVITIES INCLUDE
   SCIENCE FAIR PROJECT IDEAS.

INTRODUCTION

Have you ever stopped to think about all the ways we encounter physics in our daily life? In these projects, you'll see how trail mix uses the "Brazil Nut Effect," find out how soap can move a raft, and discover if your center of mass makes it harder or easier to pick up a piece of candy—all with physics in mind!

Projects marked with ⚛ include a section called Science Fair Project Ideas. These ideas can help you develop your own original science fair project. Science fair judges tend to reward creative thought and imagination, and it helps if you are really interested in your project. You will also need to follow the scientific method. See page 61 for more information about that.

How Empty is an Empty Bottle?

GO WITH THE FLOW: LEARN HOW INVISIBLE POCKETS OF AIR CAN HAVE A SURPRISINGLY POWERFUL EFFECT!

Did you know that airplanes and sound have something in common? Can you guess what it might be? Air pressure! It is fascinating how air—something that is so fluid and invisible—can power an amazing number of phenomena. In this activity, you will use your own breath to blow a small paper ball into an empty bottle. It sounds simple—but is it? Try it out and see for yourself!

PROJECT TIME

10 to 15 minutes

KEY CONCEPTS

Physics
Pressure
Bernoulli's principle
Air flow

5

BACKGROUND

Deep space has areas that are entirely empty—void of all matter. Scientists call this absence of matter a vacuum. On Earth, a cup or bottle can seem empty, but it is different than in truly empty space. There is not actually a vacuum inside of these containers, but air. Air is invisible to the human eye but is actually made of tiny particles that move around.

When left undisturbed, air (which is a gas) will try to create an equilibrium, meaning it will try to equalize the distribution and movement of its particles. This gets interesting when you create a disturbance, such as the wing of an airplane passing through air or a vibrating drum rhythmically pushing air particles together. In the 18th century, the Swiss scientist Daniel Bernoulli noticed that places with fast-moving air had lower air pressure compared with places where the air moves slower. As the air strives to reestablish the equilibrium, air will automatically try to move from the area with higher pressure to the area with lower pressure. This creates the lifting push on the airplane wing, the drumming sound, and other phenomena.

Could a difference in air pressure make blowing a paper ball into an "empty" bottle harder than it looks like it should be? Try the activity to find out!

MATERIALS

- A 4-by-4-inch (10-by-10-cm) piece of printer paper
- Plastic wide-mouth bottle, roughly 17 to 27 ounces (500 to 800 ml) in size. (Use a 2-by-4-inch [5-by-10-cm] piece of paper to create the ball if you only have bottles with a regular opening.)
- Table or other flat surface
- Carboard tube, such as from a paper towel roll
- Helper
- Small balls (optional)
- Other bottles or jars (optional)
- Drinking straw (optional)

PREPARATION

- Crumple the piece of paper into a tight ball. The ball should easily pass through the opening of the bottle.

PROCEDURE

● Lay the bottle on its side with its mouth facing you. Ask a helper to hold the mouth down so it touches the work surface.

● Place the paper ball in front of the bottle's mouth, about 1 inch (2.5 cm) away from the bottle.

● In a moment you will blow the ball into the bottle. *How challenging do you expect this to be?*

● Try it out! *Is it as you expected?*

● Switch places with your helper. *Can they blow the ball in the bottle?*

● Brainstorm ideas that can make blowing the ball in the bottle easier. Try out the ones that sound most promising. *If some work, what do you think makes these solutions effective whereas others fail?*

● Looking at a similar situation might help explain why it is surprisingly hard to blow a paper ball into a bottle. Try rolling the ball into the bottle. *Is that difficult? What is different when you roll a ball compared with when you blow a ball?*

● Lay the cardboard tube with an opening facing you. Place the paper ball about 1 inch (2.5 cm) in front of the tube's opening. *How challenging do you expect blowing the ball into the tube will be?*

● Try it out. *Is it as you expected?*

● Compare the tube with the bottle. *What is different and what is similar? What difference could make it more difficult to blow the ball in the bottle? Can you find ways to test your explanation?*

EXTRA

Look for other small balls or make them with items you find around the house. *Is it easier with a heavier or lighter ball?*

OBSERVATIONS AND RESULTS ········

It was probably almost impossible to blow the ball into the bottle without using a tool—but easy to blow it into the tube or roll it into the bottle.

Although the bottle and the tube seem empty, both are filled with air. The air in the tube can freely flow out at both ends of the tube, whereas the air in the bottle can only leave through its mouth.

When you blow you create a current of air, and the movement of air can take a light ball with it. When you blow toward the tube the air in front of the tube pushes the air that is already in the tube out on the other end. The ball follows the flow of air and enters the tube. When you blow toward the mouth of a bottle it is as if the air you blow and the ball following this flow of air bounce off the air that is already inside the bottle—because that inside air has nowhere to go. The ball does not enter the bottle.

You can also use Bernoulli's observation to explain why blowing the ball does not push the ball into the bottle. The air inside the bottle is moving slowly, so it is at a higher pressure compared with the fast-moving air in front of the bottle (the air you just blew). Because air always tries to reach equilibrium, the air from the bottle (the high-pressure region) will flow out of the bottle toward the low-pressure region and take the ball with it.

When you roll the ball into the bottle, air can simultaneously move out of the bottle through the bottle mouth while the ball is rolling in. In order to successfully blow the ball into the bottle, you need to concentrate the air you blow onto the ball—instead of letting the air go around it. A drinking straw can help you do that.

CLEANUP ·····················

Recycle the paper, plastic bottle, and cardboard tube. Throw away any garbage. Return all materials to the places where you found them.

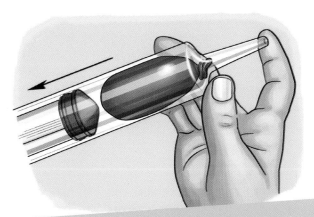

In and Out
Demonstrating Boyle's Law

UNDER PRESSURE: LEARN HOW OUR LUNGS USE PHYSICS TO HELP US BREATHE EASILY.

You have probably opened a soda before and had the liquid fizz right up out of the bottle, creating a huge mess. Why does that happen? It has to do with the carbon dioxide gas that is added to the liquid to make it fizzy. Opening the bottle releases the built-up pressure inside, causing the gas-liquid mixture to rush out of the bottle. In this activity, you will demonstrate—with the help of air- and water-filled balloons—how a gas changes volume depending on its pressure.

PROJECT TIME

10 to 15 minutes

KEY CONCEPTS

Physics
Gas
Pressure
Volume
Boyle's Law

9

BACKGROUND

The difference between solids, liquids, and gases is how the particles (molecules or atoms) behave. Particles in solids are usually tightly packed in a regular pattern. Although the particles in a liquid are also close together, they are able to move freely. Gas particles, however, are widely spread out and occupy lots of space. They continue to spread to any space that is available. This means that in contrast to liquids and solids, the volume of a gas is not fixed. Robert Boyle, a chemist and physicist from the 17th century, discovered that the volume of gas, meaning how much space it occupies, is related to its pressure—and vice versa. He found that if you pressurize a gas, its volume contracts. If you decrease its pressure, its volume increases.

You can observe a real-life application of Boyle's Law when you fill your bike tires with air. When you pump air into a tire, the gas molecules inside the tire get compressed and packed closer together. This increases the pressure of the gas, and it starts to push against the walls of the tire. You can feel how the tire becomes pressurized and tighter. Another example is a soda bottle. To get carbon dioxide gas into the liquid, the whole bottle is usually pressurized with gas. As long as the bottle is closed, it is very hard to squeeze, as the gas is confined to a small space and pushes against the bottle's walls. When you remove the cap, however, the available volume increases and some of the gas escapes. At the same time, its pressure decreases.

One important demonstration of Boyle's law is our own breathing. Inhaling and exhaling basically means increasing and decreasing the volume of our chest cavity. This creates low pressure and high pressure in our lungs, resulting in air getting sucked into our lungs and leaving our lungs. In this activity, you will create your own demonstration of Boyle's law.

MATERIALS

- At least two small balloons such as water balloons
- Scissors
- Water

- Large plastic syringe (approximately 60 milliliters works well), such as a children's oral medicine syringe (available at most drug stores). Ensure that it is airtight and does not have a needle.

PREPARATION

- Use the syringe to fill one balloon with a little bit of air—so that the balloon will still fit inside of the syringe. Tie off the balloon and trim any extra balloon material beyond the knot.

- Fill the syringe with water.

- Use the syringe to fill another balloon with some of the water, making it the same size as the air-filled balloon. Tie its opening with a knot, and trim any remaining material after the knot.

- Remove the plunger from the syringe so that it is open on the large end.

PROCEDURE

- Place the air-filled balloon just inside the large opening at the back of the syringe. Insert the plunger into the syringe, and try to push the balloon into the tip of the syringe. *How hard is it to push the plunger in? What happens to the air inside the syringe?*

- Pull the plunger back again, and move the balloon into the middle of the syringe. Then close the front opening (the tip) of the syringe with one finger, and push the plunger into the syringe again. *What do you notice? How does the balloon look or change when you push the plunger in?*

- Release your finger from the tip of the syringe. Place the balloon into the tip of the syringe, and push the plunger into the syringe until it touches the balloon. Then close the tip of the syringe with your finger and pull the plunger all the way back. *Does the balloon shape change? If yes, how? Can you explain why?*

- Replace the air-filled balloon inside the syringe with the water-filled balloon. Then place the plunger into the syringe. Close the tip of the syringe with your finger, and push the plunger into the syringe as far as you can. *How does the balloon change this time?*

11

- Release your finger from the tip of the syringe, and push the plunger all the way into the syringe until it touches the balloon at the tip of the syringe. Then close the tip of the syringe again with your finger, and try to pull the plunger back as far as you can. *What happens to the water-filled balloon? Does it behave differently than the air-filled balloon? If yes, how and why?*

ExTRA

Use the same setup, but this time add water to your syringe in addition to the air-filled and water-filled balloons. Then close the tip of the syringe and try to press the plunger into the syringe and pull it out again. *What happens this time? How does the water inside the syringe make a difference?*

OBSERVATIONS AND RESULTS ·········

Did you see the air inside the air-filled balloon contract and expand? Without closing the tip of the syringe with your finger, you can easily push on the plunger. The air can escape through the opening at the tip of the syringe. But when you close the syringe with your finger the air can't escape anymore. If you press on the plunger, you increase the pressure of the air and thus the air in the balloon contracts or decreases its volume. You should have seen the air-filled balloon shrivel up and get smaller in size. The opposite happens when you close the opening of the syringe and pull the plunger back. This time you decrease the pressure of the air inside the syringe—and its volume increases. As a result, the air-filled balloon expands and grows in size: a perfect demonstration of Boyle's law!

The results look different with the water-filled balloon. Although you are compressing the air inside the syringe when pressing on the plunger, the water inside the balloon does not get compressed. The balloon stays the same size. The water balloon also keeps its shape when pulling out the plunger while closing the tip of the syringe. In contrast to gases, liquids are not compressible as their particles are already very close together. Boyle's law only applies to gases.

If you filled the syringe with water as well, you should still have seen the air-filled balloon shrinking while pushing the plunger into the syringe. The air-filled balloon also should have expanded when pulling the plunger out while the tip of the syringe was closed. You might have noticed, though, that you were not able to push and pull the plunger in and out as far as you could with the air-filled syringe. This is again because of the fact that liquids cannot be compressed like gases. You should have observed that also when trying to push the plunger in or pull it back in the water-filled syringe with the water-filled balloon. It was probably impossible to move the plunger in and out!

CLEANUP ·················

Throw away the balloons. Put away all your other materials.

All Mixed Up?
Discover the Brazil Nut Effect

SHAKE IT UP! CAN YOU MIX SIMPLE INGREDIENTS BY SHAKING THEM TOGETHER? THE ANSWER MIGHT SURPRISE YOU.

PROJECT TIME
 10 to 15 minutes

KEY CONCEPTS
Physics
Materials
Mixture
Buoyancy

Have you ever noticed that the dried fruits or nuts in your breakfast cereal are not evenly spread out inside the box—or that in a container of mixed nuts, Brazil nuts gather at the top? This phenomenon is commonly called the "Brazil nut effect," and the science behind it is surprisingly complex and far-reaching. This situation can be a nuisance when you want to fill silos, bags, or bins with different types of materials. It can also be used to our advantage: an avalanche airbag uses the Brazil nut effect to keep skiers on top of the snow during an avalanche. In this activity, you will challenge yourself to mix different kinds of granular materials. It's not as easy as it sounds!

15

BACKGROUND ●

We encounter three states of matter: solid, liquid, and gas. We know that rocks are solid, the water in the ocean is liquid, and the air we breathe is gas. But classification is not always that clear when it comes to the way some materials behave. You can pile sand like a solid, but you can also pour it so it flows more like a liquid. This is because it is a granular material, which is made up of many individual particles, with each particle being a grain.

Granular materials can range in size from small grains, such as sand, to very large objects, such as boulders. For a granular material to show characteristics of a liquid, there must be many grains close together. A couple of boulders rolling down a hill are not acting like a liquid, but thousands of boulders tumbling together down a hill during a landslide are. Similarly, a grain of sand on its own does not act like a liquid, but it can flow more like a liquid when you pour a bunch of it out of a pail.

If you put different granular materials in a container, you could shake the container or rotate it to mix them. The shaking or rotating motions make the grains jump up or roll over each other. As smaller grains fall through the spaces between larger grains, large particles tend to move toward the top in a process called percolation. Buoyancy also plays a role: it makes denser grains sink and less dense grains float to the top. Another contributing factor is granular convection, which is when granular materials that are vibrated move in convection-like circulation patterns. The larger, denser pieces follow the circulation pattern up, and don't move down. Even the air between the particles and the container's shape are believed to make an impact.

MATERIALS ～～～～～～～

- Small transparent cylindrical container with a lid. (Small food containers work well, as do petri dishes.)
- Single color of dessert sprinkles—enough to fill your container 1/3 full
- Fine-grained material, such as extra-fine granular sugar or sifted dry sand (you can also use colorful sand from a craft store)—enough to fill your container 1/3 full
- Measuring spoon
- Small spoon for stirring

- Tape (if needed to secure the lid of your container)
- At least four trail mix ingredients of different sizes (such as peanuts, raisins, sunflower seeds, and dried strawberries) (optional)
- A larger container with a lid in which to make (and shake) the trail mix (optional)

PREPARATION

- Gather all of your materials in an area that can be easily cleaned if your granular materials spill.

- Add a tablespoon of sprinkles to your container, followed by about the same amount of your other granular material (sugar). Continue until your container is about 1/2 full. If needed, add tape around any openings or to secure the lid.

- *Are the sugar (or other granular material) and sprinkles in your container well mixed? What do you think will happen if you shake your container up and down or from side to side?*

PROCEDURE

- Move your container up and down: first slowly and then gradually faster. Observe what happens. *When do the sugar and sprinkles start moving inside the container? Do the sugar and sprinkles mix or separate when you shake the container?*

- Open your container and use the small spoon to mix the sprinkles into the sugar. Close your container and reapply tape if needed.

- Move your container from side to side, first slowly and then gradually faster. Observe what happens. *At what point do the sugar and sprinkles start to move inside the container? Do the sugar and sprinkles separate when you shake the container slowly? Do they separate when you shake the container vigorously? Why do you think this happens?*

17

- Open your container, and use the small spoon to mix the sprinkles into the sugar. Close your container and reapply tape if needed.

- Next you will rotate your container. *Do you think the mixture will stay well mixed, or mix better by this movement?*

- Try it out! *What do you observe? Why do you think this happens?*

- Move your container in whatever way you like. *Can you move your container in a way that mixes your sprinkles into the sugar?*

 ## SCIENCE FAIR IDEA

Make trail mix. Start with two ingredients, such as peanuts and raisins, and shake the container. *How well do these mix?* Add a third and then a fourth ingredient, such as sunflower seeds and freeze-dried strawberries. *How well do all of the ingredients mix when shaken? What about rolled or poured?* Try different ingredients. *Which combinations mix well? Do more ingredients make a better-mixed trail mix?*

OBSERVATIONS AND RESULTS ·········

Regardless of the way you moved your container, as soon as you moved it vigorously enough, the sprinkles and sugar probably separated.

Fine sugar grains are much smaller than sprinkles, and they might be denser too. If you shook the container vigorously enough, the particles inside probably started to jump up or glide alongside and over one another. The small sugar grains fell through small cracks between sprinkles, so the large sprinkles collected at the top and sides of your container. Moving the container did not help to mix the grains inside.

The separation and patterns are pretty, but this separation can be annoying when you want your trail mix or nuts to stay mixed!

CLEANUP ·····························

18

Store or eat the trail mix. Throw away your sugar and sprinkles mix, or find a use for them. Return all materials to the places where you found them.

Make Your Own Spring Scale

WHY GUESS A WEIGHT WHEN YOU CAN MAKE A SCALE? LEARN HOW SOME SCALES USE A SPRING TO MEASURE THE MASS OF OBJECTS—AND BUILD YOUR VERY OWN!

Have you ever played with a Slinky, used a pinball machine, written with a click pen, or ridden in a car? If so, then you have made use of a spring! Springs are in machines all around us and have many useful purposes. In this activity, you will learn another cool use for a spring: making a scale to weigh objects.

PROJECT TIME
15 to 20 minutes

KEY CONCEPTS
Springs
Elasticity
Weight
Distance

BACKGROUND

Springs are usually spirals made from metal. They have the useful property that they are very stretchy—the scientific term for this is elastic. If you squish a spring or pull on it, then let go, it will bounce back to its original shape. There are limits to this behavior, however. If you pull (or push) too much, you might take the spring past its elastic limit. After that point, there will be some permanent change—or deformation—in the spring, and it will not recover its original shape.

Luckily, the elastic behavior of a spring is defined by a well-known equation called Hooke's law, which states that the restoring force of a spring (how hard the spring pushes or pulls to get back to its original length) is proportional to the distance the spring has been stretched (or compressed) from its original length. This law is expressed mathematically as $F = kx$, where F is force, x is the spring's change in length, and k is a number called the spring constant, which is different for springs of different sizes or materials. For a given spring, however, k remains the same as long as you stay within the spring's elastic limit. This makes Hooke's law useful because if you can measure either the force or change in length, you can use the spring constant to calculate the other value.

You might think of a scale as something that you stand—or place objects—on, measuring mass pushing down on it. But you can also weigh objects from a hanging scale, in which mass pulls on it. In this project, you will make a simple spring scale by hanging weights from a spring. First you have to calibrate the scale using known weights, but after that you can measure the weight of an unknown object by hanging it from the spring, and measuring how far the spring stretches.

MATERIALS

- A spring (You can find a selection of springs at a hardware store or get one by disassembling a click pen or some toys—with permission, of course. Ask an adult to help you take apart a pen or toy if necessary.)
- Paper clips
- Small plastic bucket or a paper or plastic cup with string tied through holes near the top to form a handle
- Kitchen scale
- Ruler

- Objects to use as weights, such as coins (The weight of the objects you use will depend on how strong your spring is.)
- Paper and pencil or pen
- Various small household objects to measure

PROCEDURE

- Play with your spring using your hands to get a sense for how strong it is. *How hard do you have to push on it to compress it? How hard do you have to pull on it to stretch it out?* Be careful not to push or pull on it so hard that you go past its elastic limit and permanently deform it, but this should give you a good idea of how heavy your weights should be.

- Hang your spring vertically from one of the paper clips by hooking the second coil of the spring with an end of the paper clip. (You might want to bend the end of the paper clip out a bit to make it easier to hook the spring.) You can hold the paper clip with your hand—or clip it on to something such as a hook, if available.

- Use the ruler to measure the length of the spring with no weight hanging from it. Write this number down.

- Now, use a second paper clip, looped onto the second-from-the-bottom coil, to hang your bucket or cup from the bottom of the spring.

- Add a few weights (such as coins) to the bucket or cup. Add enough weight that the spring stretches out a bit and you can measure a change in length. Exactly how much you need to add to see a change will depend on your spring. Be careful not to add so much weight that you stretch the spring past its elastic limit and permanently deform it. *How does the spring stretch as you add weight?*

- Measure the new length of the spring and write this number down.

- Remove the bucket or cup from the spring and weigh it, including the weights, using the kitchen scale. Write this number down next to the distance you just measured.

- Repeat this process and add a few more weights to the bucket or cup. Write down the new length of the spring and the new weight.

- Repeat the measurement a few more times until you have a few data points. Be careful not to add too much weight and permanently stretch the spring. *What happens to the distance as you keep adding weight?*

- Now, try to figure out the weight of another object without using your kitchen scale. *Can you do it using the data from the experiment you just did?*

- Hang the object from your spring and measure how far the spring stretches. Then, compare this distance with the distances you recorded during your experiment and look up the corresponding weight. (This will be easier if you have a graph; see first "Extra" below.) *How much does the object weigh according to your data? Now measure it on the kitchen scale—how close were you?*

- Repeat this process with a few more objects and compare the weights you look up using your spring scale with what you measure with your kitchen scale. *How accurate is your scale?* If it's good enough, perhaps you can keep it around for use in the kitchen or for other activities!

ExTRA
Make a graph of your data, with distance on the x axis and weight on the y axis. This will make it easier to determine the weight of other objects. *Is your graph a straight line?*

ExTRA
Using Hooke's law and your data, can you calculate the spring constant, k, for your spring? Hint: k is the slope of a graph of force versus distance.

OBSERVATIONS AND RESULTS ·········

The exact weights and distances you measure will depend on the individual spring. But in general you'll see that any spring follows Hooke's law within its elastic limit. That means the relationship between weight and distance is linear—if you double the weight, the amount the spring stretches will double. For example, say your spring has an unstretched length of 10 centimeters. When you add a certain amount of weight, it stretches to 11 centimeters (a change of 1 centimeter from its unstretched length). When you add double that weight, it should stretch to 12 centimeters (a change of 2 centimeters from its unstretched length).

Once you have collected a few data points, this allows you to easily "look up" the weight of a new object simply by using a ruler to measure the change in the spring's length. This is how real spring scales work—the springs are calibrated so that when they are stretched by a certain amount, it corresponds to a known weight. This fails, however, if you stretch a spring beyond its elastic limit. That will cause some permanent change in the spring's shape, so it will not return to its original length and your measurements are no longer valid.

CLEANUP ················

Return all materials to the places where you found them.

Separation by Distillation

CAN YOU SEPARATE THE INGREDIENTS OF A SOLUTION JUST USING HEAT? TRY THIS SWEET ACTIVITY AND FIND OUT!

PROJECT TIME
 60 to 75 minutes

KEY CONCEPTS

Physics
Boiling point
Condensation
Distillation

Do you like cooking? If you have helped in the kitchen at home or watched someone else cook, you have probably seen lots of liquids—such as water, milk, and soup—heated. Did you notice that once the liquid boils, a lot of steam develops? Have you ever wondered what the steam is made of and what happens to all the substances such as sugar or salt that are dissolved in the solution you are boiling? Do they boil off too, or do they stay behind in the solution? In this activity, you will build a distillation device that allows you to sample the steam that you generate while boiling fruit juice! How do you think it will taste?

25

BACKGROUND

What do you need to make a solution? First, you need water or a solvent and then you need a substance such as sugar or salt to dissolve, also called the solute. The solvent and solute become one solution—a homogeneous mixture—in which you cannot see the difference between them anymore. Most solutions actually contain many different substances. But what if you want to separate the individual components from a liquid solution? There is a process called distillation that allows you to do just that. It is used in many real-world applications, such as making medicine, perfumes, or some food products.

Distillation exploits the differences in the volatility of the solution's components, which means every compound has a different boiling point and starts to vaporize (change from its liquid to gaseous state) at a different temperature. When distilling, you heat up the solution so that the component with the lowest boiling point evaporates first, leaving the other solutes behind. The vaporized component in the gaseous state can then be collected in a different container by condensation and is called distillate. This means that the vapor is cooled down so the gas becomes a liquid again. By changing the distillation temperature, you can separate many different substances according to their different volatilities. If you have a solution that includes a nonvolatile solute, however, this compound will always stay behind in the solution.

Knowing now how distillation works, what do you think will happen to the fruit juice once you heat it? Make your own distillation device and find out!

MATERIALS

- Stove (Always work with an adult helper when using the stove.)
- Deep cooking pot with sloped lid (transparent lid, if you have one)
- Ceramic bowl
- Small ceramic plate or ceramic coffee cup
- Three glasses
- Apple or cranberry juice (about 2 cups [0.5 l])
- Liquid measuring cup
- Ice
- Oven mitts
- Broth (optional)
- Cooking thermometer (optional)
- Vinegar (optional)

PREPARATION

- Make sure all of your materials are clean. (Then you will be able to sample the juice and products at the end of the activity.)

- Place the small ceramic plate in the center of the cooking pot. Depending on how deep your pot is, you can also place a ceramic coffee cup in its center.

- Place a ceramic bowl on top of the small plate or coffee cup.

- Put your pot on the stove.

PROCEDURE

- Measure out and pour 1 cup (240 ml) of the fruit juice into a glass. *Have a look at its color and take a small sip to taste it. Is it very sweet? How does the color look; is it very intense?* Keep the rest of the juice for comparison at the end.

- Pour another 1 cup (240 ml) of colored fruit juice in the bottom of the pot. (Your small ceramic plate or ceramic coffee cup will now be standing in the juice.)

- Together with your adult helper, turn on the stove to medium heat and bring the juice to a boil. It should be a moderate rather than a rolling boil. *Can you see the steam developing once your juice starts boiling?*

- Now place the cover on the pot, upside down, so that the tip of the sloping lid is facing toward the bowl placed inside the pot. *What happens to the steam once you close the lid?*

- Put ice in the cover of the pot. You might have to replace the ice in the lid as it melts. *If you use a transparent lid, can you see droplets forming on the inward-facing side of the lid? Where do they come from and what happens to the droplets?*

- Allow the juice to boil for 20 to 30 minutes, making sure some juice always remains in the bottom of the pot. *Do you see any changes in the amount of juice inside the pot?*

27

- After 20 to 30 minutes, turn the burner off. Allow the pot to cool for a few minutes.

- Put on oven mitts and carefully remove the cover from the pot. *What do you notice about the empty bowl that you placed under the lid?*

- Still wearing oven mitts, lift the bowl off the small ceramic plate or coffee cup and set it down on a heat-resistant surface.

- Remove the small plate or coffee cup. *Looking at the remaining juice in the pot, is there more or less juice left than the amount you poured in?*

- After it cools, pour the remaining juice from the pot into a glass. *Did the juice change during boiling? What is different?*

- Pour the cooled distillate (the condensed steam), which is now the liquid inside the small bowl, into a glass. *How does the distillate look?*

- Now take the glass from the beginning with the original juice, and place it next to the remaining juice and distillate. Compare their appearances. *How do they differ? Did you expect these results? Why do you think the juice changed the way it did? How much fruit juice is left compared with what you poured into the pot?*

- Let the liquids cool to room temperature. Because you used clean kitchen utensils and edible fruit juice in this experiment, go ahead and take a sip of each of the solutions. *How do the three different liquids compare in taste? Which one is the sweetest? Which one is the least sweet? How does the condensed steam taste? Why do you think there is a difference?*

- Finally, recombine the distillate and the remaining fruit juice by pouring the distillate into the remaining fruit juice. *Do the volumes add up to what you put in at the beginning? How do the appearance and taste of this solution compare with the original fruit juice?*

SCIENCE FAIR IDEA

Repeat this activity with a salty solution, such as broth, instead of the sweet fruit juice. *Do you think the results will be similar? What happens to the salt in the broth when you are boiling it?*

 SCIENCE FAIR IDEA

Try to do this experiment again with household vinegar. Vinegar is a mixture of about 4 to 6 percent acetic acid and water. *Can you separate these two liquids by distillation? How does your distillate taste in this case?*

EXTRA

You might know that the boiling temperature of pure water is 212°F (100°C) at normal atmospheric pressure. Adding a solute such as sugar, salt, or other compounds to water will change the boiling point of the resulting solution. Try heating up your three liquids (original juice, distillate, and remaining juice) and measure their boiling points with a thermometer. *Are they very different? How does the boiling point change with increasing solute concentration?*

OBSERVATIONS AND RESULTS ·········

Juices are usually very sweet. This is because fruits contain a lot of fruit sugar, called fructose. More than 80 percent of most fruits, however, consist of water, so basically the apple or cranberry juice is a mixture of water and sugar. Once you reach the boiling point of the juice, it will start to evaporate and you will see steam coming out of the pot. If you close the pot with a lid, the steam rises up to the lid, and because the lid is much colder than the steam (especially after you put the ice on top), the vapor cools down rapidly and it condenses, becoming a liquid again that you can see in the form of droplets inside the lid. These droplets fall and are collected in the bowl that you have placed in the pot. As the juice boiled, you probably noticed that the amount of water in the bowl increased whereas the amount of juice in the pot decreased. This is because the steam, which was part of the juice, was collected in a separate container. If combined, the distillate and the remaining juice should add up to a similar volume of juice that you had in the beginning.

29

When you compared the three different solutions at the end (original juice, distillate, and remaining juice), the first thing you probably saw was that the color of the remaining juice became much darker and the distillate had no color at all and looked like pure water. And it actually is pure water; it shouldn't have had any sweetness when you tasted it whereas the remaining juice should have tasted much sweeter than the original juice. The reason for this is that sugar is a nonvolatile compound, which means that when you boil any sugary liquid, the sugar will stay behind in the solution and not be transferred into a gaseous state. The water component of the mixture, however, starts to evaporate at about 212°F (100°C), resulting in a steam consisting of pure water. Salt is also a nonvolatile substance and if you repeated the activity with broth, your distillate also should have been pure water. If you compared the boiling points of all three solutions at the end, you might have noticed that you can increase water's boiling point by adding solutes—the higher the amount of solutes, the higher its boiling point will be.

Vinegar, on the other hand—or a mixture of 4 to 6 percent acetic acid and water—is not easily separable by distillation. This is because the boiling points of water (212°F [100°C]) and vinegar (about 213°F [100.6°C]) are too close together to result in a full separation of both components. You should have noticed that the distillate still tasted like vinegar.

CLEANUP ·························

Dispose of any remaining juice. Wash all dishes.
Put away all materials.

Surface Tension Science
Build a Raft Powered by Soap

CAN DISH SOAP HELP MOVE A RAFT?
FIND OUT IN THIS EXPERIMENT!

Have you ever wondered why a water strider bug can walk on water? Would you believe it is based on the same reasons soap can clean your dishes? In fact, if you look around you carefully, you can find dozens of interesting phenomena that depend on the surface tension of water. In this science activity, you will make a little raft that is actually powered by surface tension—and use your vessel to investigate how surface tension works!

PROJECT TIME
15 to 20 minutes

KEY CONCEPTS
Physics
Energy
Liquids
Molecules
Surface tension

BACKGROUND

If you've ever blown up different types of balloons, you know it's pretty easy to blow up a balloon made of thin, soft, stretchy rubber. That is because the balloon offers little resistance to becoming stretched out as it's blown up. But for a balloon made of thicker or stiffer rubber, more energy is required to inflate it. The balloon is more resistant to stretching and can be a model for surface tension. How "stretchy" the balloon material is determines how much resistance (or, in this case, surface tension) must be overcome by your breath to inflate it. Surface tension is defined as the energy needed to increase a surface area by a certain amount.

Liquids also have surface tension. The liquid's molecules (small particles) are constantly pushing and pulling against one another with tiny electric charges. When a water molecule is surrounded by other water molecules, pulling forces are balanced by pushing forces, so it's not pulled in one direction more than any other. But at the surface, where air and water meet, that's not true; water molecules there get pulled down, toward other water molecules, more than up, toward the air. This causes the surface tension of water.

MATERIALS

- Scissors
- A small, flat piece of Styrofoam, at least about 3 by 3 inches (7.6 by 7.6 cm) (For example, this could be part of a take-out container or a sheet of packaging.)
- Utility or EXACTO knife and an adult helper to use it
- Kitchen sponge (Use either a fresh sponge or rinse the sponge thoroughly with water to make sure it does not have any soap in it.)

- Toothpick
- Large basin, sink, or bathtub
- Liquid dish soap or liquid laundry detergent
- Water
- Medicine dropper (optional)
- Ruler (optional)

PREPARATION ·······················

- With an adult's help, cut the Styrofoam piece into a small rectangular shape, such as one about 3 by 2 inches (7.6 by 5 cm) or 4 by 3 inches (10.2 by 7.6 cm). This will be your raft. If you want, you can make it a different shape than a rectangle, so long as it is symmetrical, not longer than about 6 inches (15.2 cm) and has a flat area on one side that's at least 2 inches (5 cm) long.

- On one of the short ends of the raft (or the flat area that is at least 2 inches [5 cm]) long), about 1/2 inch (1.3 cm) in from the end of the raft, take a utility knife and carefully cut out a square about 1 by 1 inch (2.5 by 2.5 cm) in size. Center the square along that end. This will be the back of the raft.

- Again, with an adult's help, cut a small square of the kitchen sponge, about 1 by 1 inch (2.5 by 2.5 cm) in size. This sponge piece should fit in the square you cut out of the raft, so adjust the size of the sponge piece if needed. *How do you think the sponge will power your raft?*

- Run a toothpick horizontally through the sponge piece. The toothpick will rest on the Styrofoam raft, whereas the sponge will rest in the raft's square hole. Run the toothpick closer to the top side of the sponge so that when you place it in the Styrofoam hole, the bottom of the sponge piece is at least as low as the bottom of the Styrofoam raft. *Why do you think it's important that the sponge touches the water?*

- Now, with an adult's help, cut out the small remaining strip of Styrofoam between the square and that end of the raft, but make the cutout not as wide as the sponge. For example, if your sponge piece is 1 inch (2.5 cm) on each side, only about 1/2 inch (1.3 cm) or 3/4 inch (1.9 cm) of the Styrofoam strip should be cut away. (This is because when you place your raft in the water, you will want the sponge piece to have some open water behind it, but part of the Styrofoam strip needs to still be there to prevent the sponge from floating away.) Your raft is now ready to sail!

33

PROCEDURE

- Fill a large basin, sink, or bathtub with water. Make sure there's enough room for your raft to move around.

- Once the water has settled, put the raft onto the water surface and let it float. Make sure the sponge piece stays in the raft's square cutout.

- Once the raft is not moving, carefully put one or two drops of liquid dish soap or laundry detergent on the sponge piece. Make sure none of the detergent accidentally drops into the water. If needed, you could use a medicine dropper to better aim the drops. *What happens to the raft when detergent is placed on the sponge? How does it move?*

- If you want to observe the motion again, empty the basin, rinse the raft (especially the sponge) to get all of the detergent out of it and refill the basin. Test the raft again, as you did before.

- *Knowing that detergents decrease water's surface tension, can you use this fact to explain why the raft moves this way?*

⚛ SCIENCE FAIR IDEA

You could repeat this activity but test substances other than detergent to see whether they affect the surface tension. For example, you could try different soaps, toothpaste, vegetable oil, table salt, etcetera. *Do other substances affect surface tension, and the motion of the raft, in the same way that the liquid dish soap does?*

EXTRA

You could try changing the size or shape of the raft and repeat the experiment. *How does using a raft that is a different shape or heavier or lighter affect how the raft travels using surface tension?*

34

EⅹTRA

Think about how you could change the design of your raft to improve it. *Can you alter its design so that it goes faster or straighter?*

OBSERVATIONS AND RESULTS ·········

Did the raft move forward, away from the end where the sponge piece was placed?

You should have seen that when you added a drop or two of detergent on the sponge piece of the raft, the raft should have quickly moved away from the side where the detergent was added, propelling it forward through the water.

When detergent is added to water, it decreases the surface tension of the water. Compounds that lower water's surface tension are called surfactants, which work by separating the water molecules from one another. In this activity, the surface tension is lowered in the area where the surfactant is added, and the higher surface tension in front of the raft pulls the raft forward. As the detergent spreads through the water, it decreases the surface tension throughout the water, and the raft stops moving eventually because there is no longer a difference in the surface tension. How do you think a surfactant such as dish soap helps to clean dirty dishes?

CLEANUP ················

Dump any remaining water down the drain. Throw away any garbage. Return all materials to the places where you found them.

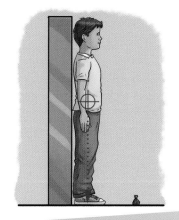

Balancing Challenges

FIND YOUR CENTER—OF MASS. LEARN A LITTLE ABOUT PHYSICS—AND YOURSELF—WITH THESE SIMPLE PHYSICAL CHALLENGES!

Did you ever come across a challenge that looked almost too easy to try—but turned out to be surprisingly difficult, if not impossible? This activity challenges you in a fun way. Something as simple as picking up a piece of candy can be way harder than it looks. Find out why some movements are harder than you'd expect, and then trick your friends into trying them. Astonish them with your stunning knowledge of the laws of physics—but most of all, have fun!

PROJECT TIME
10 to 15 minutes

KEY CONCEPTS
Physics
Balance
Gravity
Center of mass

BACKGROUND

Gravity is a force that acts between any two masses, but you only notice it if at least one of the masses is huge, such as the mass of Earth at about 1.317×10^{25} pounds (5.97×10^{24} kilograms). We encounter the effects of Earth's gravity daily. Gravity prevents you from floating off into space when you jump, makes objects fall to the ground when you release them, and makes it difficult to hold your balance on one foot without falling over. When balancing or jumping, gravity acts on us as if all our body's mass is squished into one point and gravity pulls on that point. The point is called the center of mass, and how the body's mass is distributed determines its location. If you are a child, your center of mass is usually below the belly button when you are standing. Wearing a heavy backpack will shift your center of mass up because more mass is now located on the upper part of your body. Leaning to the left moves part of your mass to the left so your center of mass shifts to the left as well. Similarly, leaning forward moves it forward. As you grow, your mass distribution changes and the center of mass shifts accordingly. It tends to stay low for adult females whereas in most adult males their center of mass is above the belly button when standing.

Why is this important? If our center of mass is directly above whatever supports us (our feet, a chair, etcetera) we feel balanced. If it is not, we feel unbalanced and need to do something or else we will topple over and fall. The challenges in this science activity allow you to experience this. Go ahead, feel it for yourself!

MATERIALS

- Wall to lean against
- Partner
- Candy in a wrapper
- Ruler (optional)
- Chair without armrests and a straight back (optional)

PREPARATION

- Gather your materials and bring your partner to the location where you will perform the test.

PROCEDURE

- Stand with your back against a wall with your heels touching the wall and your feet together.

- Ask your partner to put a piece of candy about 1 foot (30 cm) in front of your feet. *Do you think you could pick up the candy without bending your knees or moving your feet?*

- Try it. *Did you succeed? Was your prediction correct?*

- Stand away from the wall, with your feet together and a piece of candy again about 1 foot (30 cm) in front of your feet. *Do you think you can pick up the candy now?* Remember, you are not allowed to bend your knees or move your feet.

- Try it. *Did you succeed? Was the latter challenge easier or harder than the first one? Why would this be?*

- For the next challenge, stand tall on two feet and away from the wall. You are allowed to bend your knees but keep your arms next to your body. *Can you lift your left foot without moving your right foot? Do you think you could do this with your right side leaning against the wall?*

- Stand with your right side against the wall so your foot, hip, arm, and shoulder touch the wall. You are allowed to bend your knees. *Can you lift your left foot without moving the right foot? Why would standing against a wall make such a big difference?*

EXTRA

Sit in a chair without armrests and a straight back with your back straight up, feet flat on the ground and hands on your thighs. Now try to stand up, keeping your back vertical, hands on your thighs and feet on the ground. *Can you do it? Why would this be so hard?*

ExTRA

This challenge requires empty space behind and in front of you. Bend over to grab your toes, with your knees slightly bent. Now try to jump, first forward then backward. *Which one is easier, and why would this be the case?* Hint: Observe how your center of mass (or your mass distribution) shifts when doing a regular jump forward or backward. Think of how your mass distribution is different when bending over to hold your toes compared with standing up. *How would this impact the location of your center of mass? How could this make specific jumps difficult?*

OBSERVATIONS AND RESULTS ·········

Was it surprisingly difficult to accomplish some of these seemingly straightforward challenges?

Every person (and every solid item) has a center of mass. Where this point is located determines whether you (or the solid item) is balanced or will fall over. When you stand against the wall, your center of mass is above your feet so you are balanced. When you bend over, the mass of your head and torso moves forward. As a result, your center of mass moves forward and away from your feet; you feel you are about to lose your balance and fall over. You can save yourself by moving a foot forward so your center of mass falls in between your two feet—but that is not allowed in the challenge. It is not possible to pick up that candy! The laws of physics prevent it. Without the wall behind you, you could probably pick up the candy. Did you notice that you pushed your behind backward for counterbalance while bending over? This kept your center of mass above your feet and helped you with your balance.

A similar thing happened when you tried to stand on one foot. As you probably noticed, without the wall you could lift your left foot with ease. When you stood with your right side against the wall and tried to lift your left foot, however, you could not do it. Your center of mass was above the area spanned by your two feet. With the wall to the right of you, you had no way to shift your center of mass to the right by leaning to the right so it would be above your right foot when you lifted your left foot.

If you tried the extra challenges, you were probably stuck in your chair and unable to make a single jump forward—although backward jumps were possible. These challenges are set up so certain shifts in your center of mass are not allowed or force you to lose your balance. You were not allowed to bend forward while standing up from your chair, and leaning forward before doing a forward jump makes you lose your balance.

CLEANUP ·····················

Treat yourself to the piece of candy. Return any other materials to where you found them.

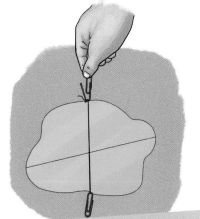

X Marks the Spot
Finding the Center of Mass

CAN YOU FIND THE CENTER OF A SHAPE? YOU'LL BE ABLE TO—EVEN FOR THE ODDEST OBLONG CREATION—WITH THIS SIMPLE SCIENCE ACTIVITY. NO STRINGS ATTACHED (OKAY, MAYBE ONE)!

With a little time, you can probably find the center of simple shapes such as circles and squares pretty easily. But how do you find the "middle" of an irregular shape such as a drawing of a dog or a cat? This project will show you how to do it using nothing but string and paper clips!

PROJECT TIME

15 to 20 minutes

KEY CONCEPTS

Physics
Geometry
Gravity
Center of mass

BACKGROUND

How do you define the exact center of an object? One way to do this is to find the object's center of mass. The center of mass is the point about which an object will balance if you try to rest it on your fingertip. Or if you hang an object, for example a picture frame from a nail, the center of mass will hang directly below the nail.

For symmetrical objects, finding the center of mass is relatively easy. For example, for a rectangular picture frame, you know the center of mass is in the middle of the rectangle and you can find that with a ruler. When you hang the picture frame, you will make sure it is centered on the nail—otherwise it will tip to one side and will be off-center. The same applies to other symmetrical objects such as a spherical basketball; you know the center of mass is in the middle of the sphere.

What about irregularly shaped objects such as a dog or cat or person? Now finding the center of mass is not so easy! This activity will show you how to find the center of mass for any two-dimensional shape you cut out of paper using a trick that has to do with the hanging picture frame mentioned above. If you hang a shape from a single point, you know the center of mass will always rest directly below that point. So, if you hang a shape from two different points (one at a time) and draw a line straight down from each point, the center of mass is where those lines intersect. This technique can be used for any irregular two-dimensional shape. Don't believe it? Try this activity to find out!

MATERIALS

- Paper (Heavier paper, such as construction paper, card stock, or thin cardboard from the side of a cereal box will work best.)
- Scissors (Have an adult help with cutting if necessary—especially on thicker materials.)
- String
- Pencil
- Ruler
- Two paper clips or a pushpin and another small, relatively heavy object you can tie to the string (such as a metal washer)

PREPARATION

- Cut a piece of string about 1 foot (30 cm) long and tie a paper clip to each end. (Alternatively, you can use any other small object such as a metal washer on one end—this will serve as a weight—and any other small, pointy object like a needle or pushpin on the other end—this will be used to puncture the paper.)

PROCEDURE

- Start with an easy shape: Cut out a rectangular piece of paper or cardboard. *Can you guess where the center of mass of the rectangle is?* If so, use a ruler to measure where you think it will be and mark this spot with your pencil.

- Punch several small holes around the edge of the paper using your paper clip (or pushpin). Make them as close to the edge as possible without ripping the paper. (This is important for the accuracy of this technique). The exact location of the holes does not matter but this technique will work best if you space them all the way around the edge (not just put two holes right next to each other).

- Now poke one end of one paper clip (or pushpin) through one of the holes to act like a hanging hook. Make sure the paper can swing easily from the hook and does not get stuck (Rotate it back and forth a few times to loosen the hole if necessary).

- Hold on to your "hook" and hold the paper up against the wall. Let the paper swing freely and make sure the string can hang straight down and does not get stuck.

- Use a pencil and ruler to draw a straight line on the paper along the string. *Does this line go through the center of mass you predicted earlier?*

- Now, hang your paper from a different hole and repeat the process. *Where does this line intersect the first line?*

45

- Repeat the process several more times with different holes. *Do all the lines intersect at the same point?*

- Now cut out an irregular shape. You can cut out a "blob" or draw something like a dog or cat and then cut out the outline. Make sure the shape you cut out remains stiff and flat. (That is, do not cut very thin sections that might be floppy.) *Can you use a ruler to predict where the center of mass of your irregular shape will be?* This is much harder!

- Punch holes around the edge of your irregular shape and repeat the activity. Hang the shape and the string from each of the holes, one at a time, and draw a line along the string. *Where do the lines intersect? Does this match up with what you predicted?*

ExtRA

If you use a stiff enough material to cut out your shape (such as cardboard), can you try balancing it on your fingertip at the center of mass? What happens if you try to balance it using another point?

OBSERVATIONS AND RESULTS ·········

You should have found that the center of mass of the rectangle is right in the middle of the piece—halfway along the width and halfway along the height. You can easily locate this spot with a ruler. Then, when you hang the rectangle from a hole on its edge, the string should always pass through this point, regardless of which hole you use. While it is much harder to predict the center of mass for an irregular shape, the same principle holds true. Regardless of what point you hang the irregular shape from, the string will always pass through the center of mass. So, if you hang it from two or more points (one at a time), you can find the intersection of these lines—and that is the center of mass.

Note that due to small variables in the activity (such as friction on the hook that prevents the paper from rotating perfectly or the holes not being close enough to the edge of the paper), if you draw multiple lines, they might not all intersect in exactly the same place but they should still be fairly close to one another.

CLEANUP ·················

Recycle any used paper or cardboard. Return all materials to the places where you found them.

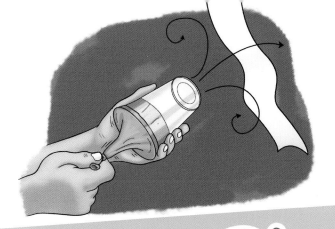

⚛ Create a Ring of Air!

LEARNING ABOUT AIR PRESSURE IS A BLAST WITH THIS FUN PHYSICS ACTIVITY!

PROJECT TIME

25 minutes

KEY CONCEPTS

Physics
Air
Pressure
Vortex
Aerodynamics

Here is a riddle for you: I am everywhere but you don't see me—what am I? The answer is: air! It is all around us, but it is usually invisible. We can, however, see the effect air has—for example when wind is moving tree branches. Air can move gently to create a nice breeze or turn into a wild and destructive hurricane. Not only can wind move objects with air, you can do it too—as long as the objects are not too heavy! You can, for example blow on something—or you can create an air cannon, which shoots big blasts of air into . . . the air! Curious how this works? Then try this activity to find out!

49

BACKGROUND

Although air is invisible, it is made up of different molecules, mostly those of oxygen, nitrogen, and carbon dioxide. When wind is blowing in your face you can actually feel these molecules press against you. But what makes them move to create wind? Air moves due to differences in air pressure. It always moves from areas of high to low air pressure. Differences in air pressure can, for example, be caused by temperature differences. You can also physically move air and create areas of high and low air pressure by "pushing" or manipulating the air around you. The investigation of how and why air flows is called the science of aerodynamics. One fascinating airflow phenomenon is a toroidal vortex, which looks like a doughnut-shaped ring of air. You rarely notice these unless there are some particles in the air such as steam or smoke, which make the vortex ring visible.

In this activity, you can create such an air vortex yourself with a self-made vortex cannon! With this device you will create a burst of air that shoots out of a hole. The fast-moving air displaces the air outside of the hole, which then swirls around in the shape of a doughnut. The air forms this shape because the air leaving the cup at the center of the hole is traveling faster than that leaving around the edge of the hole. The difference in air pressure between the fast-moving air inside the vortex ring and the slow-flowing air on the outside of it makes the vortex spin, keeping it stable while moving through the air. With some practice you can get your air vortex to move so fast that you might even be able to knock over a paper cup with it!

MATERIALS

- Disposable plastic cups (one 8-ounce [236 ml] and one 16-ounce [473 ml] size)
- Scissors
- Adult helper
- Balloons
- Toilet paper
- Duct tape
- Measuring tape
- Pen
- Paper

PREPARATION

- Hang up some strips of toilet paper by taping them to a doorframe.

- Unroll toilet paper as you use the measuring tape to measure out about 3 feet (0.9 m), 9 feet (2.7 m), and 15 feet (4.5 m) away from the doorframe. Make marks on the toilet paper at each of these distances.

- Draw a 1.5-inch (4-cm) diameter circle on the bottom of both of your cups.

- With the help of an adult, use scissors to cut out both of the circles.

- Inflate two balloons to stretch them out, then deflate them again.

- Tie a knot in the neck of the balloons, then cut off the tip of the balloon.

- Cover the top of the cup with the balloon with the tied neck facing outward.

- Make sure to tape the balloon tightly to the cup on the sides—you want an airtight seal!

PROCEDURE

- Choose the smaller cup to begin with. Practice firing the air cannon by pulling back on the knot of the balloon and releasing it. Try pulling the balloon the same distance every time to create the same amount of force that pushes the air out. *What happens if you do this? Can you hear a sound? Do you feel anything in front of the cup?*

- Stand at the 3-foot (0.9-m) mark in front of the toilet paper and shoot your air cannon aiming at the hanging toilet paper. *Does the toilet paper move? Do all of the pieces move or only some of them?*

51

- Next, move to the 9-foot (3-m) mark and shoot your air cannon at the toilet paper. *Does the toilet paper still move? More or less than at the 3-foot (0.9-m) mark?*

- Finally, go to the 15-foot (5-m) mark and again aim your air burst at the toilet paper. *Do you still see the toilet paper moving? Why or why not?*

- Change to the bigger vortex cannon and repeat the steps. *Do your results change depending on the size of your air cannon? If yes, how? Can you shoot farther with the smaller or bigger cup? Why do you think this is the case?*

 SCIENCE FAIR IDEA

Use even bigger or smaller cups to make more air cannons. *How far can you make the air vortex travel? Can you find a relationship between the size of your air cannon and the distance the air vortex travels?*

EXTRA

Try changing the size of the exit hole in the bottom of the cup. Does your air cannon behave differently with smaller or larger holes? How?

 SCIENCE FAIR IDEA

Try making a rectangular air cannon. Does a box work as well as a cup? Try it to find out!

EXTRA

What happens if you pull the balloon farther out to create a larger force pushing the air out of the cup? Does it affect how fast or far the air vortex travels?

OBSERVATIONS AND RESULTS ··········

Could you make the toilet paper move by shooting an air vortex at it? The air vortex, which is basically a blast of air, shoots out of the cup so fast that it pushes the toilet paper away, so it starts moving. The air-vortex cannon works by quickly applying force to the air molecules inside the cup. When the balloon surface snaps forward it collides directly with the air molecules inside the cup, pushing and accelerating them toward the hole at the end of the cup. This push starts a chain reaction of high-speed collisions with other air molecules, and the only way for them to escape is through the opening at the end of the cup. You should have heard the "poof" of the air escaping rapidly through the hole each time you used your air cannon.

The fast-moving air then mixes with the still air outside the cup, and a vortex is formed. Because there is a higher air pressure on the outside of the ring (as the surrounding air moves slowly) and lower pressure on the inside (as the air in the vortex moves faster) the vortex spins and stays together as it travels across the room. Eventually the doughnut-shaped ring breaks up and disappears. You should have noticed that with a larger vortex cannon it takes longer for the air vortex to disappear, meaning that it traveled farther. This is because you are able to push a larger volume of air out of the cannon. Other design criteria such as the size and shape of the exit hole or the shape of the container (cup versus box) matter too. Also, if you put more force on the membrane by pulling the balloon farther out, you make the vortex travel farther as the air gets pushed out of the cup faster.

CLEANUP ·····················
Throw away the cups, balloons, and toilet paper. Return all other materials to the places where you found them.

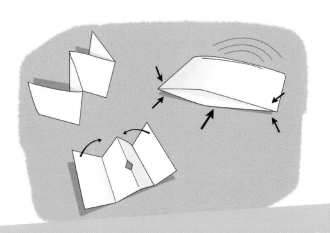

Paper Squawker

SQUAWK! LEARN HOW YOU CAN CHANGE SOUND WAVES WITH JUST A PIECE OF PAPER AND A PAIR OF SCISSORS. PHYSICS NEVER SOUNDED SO FUN(NY)!

PROJECT TIME

15 minutes

KEY CONCEPTS

Physics
Frequency
Sound waves
Pitch

Did you know that not all animals use their ears to hear sounds? Snakes, for example, perceive sound waves through their jawbones! And many insects perceive sound waves through their antennae. Although these methods of detecting sound might be different, they all respond to the same thing that our ears do, which is sound waves in the environment. In this activity, you will generate some impressive sound waves from very simple materials and observe how these sound waves are generated. Get ready to make some noise!

55

BACKGROUND

Sound reaches our ears in the form of sound waves. Similar to an ocean wave, sound waves are created by vibrations or movement in a given medium. When the wave is in the ocean, the medium is the water. In the case of sound waves, the medium that the waves travel through is the air around us. Just like an ocean wave can originate from someone jumping into the water, a sound wave originates from a vibrating object, such as a tuning fork or guitar string.

When someone jumps into the ocean they displace the water around them and cause water molecules to bump into each other. Those water molecules bump into other water molecules, and the wave is propagated through the water. In a similar manner, when a guitar string is plucked, the string vibrates, disturbing the air particles all around it. These air particles bump into air particles around them, propagating the sound wave through the air. These particles vibrate at the same frequency (or rate) as the vibration of the guitar string.

Sound waves with different frequencies sound different to our ears. We perceive higher-frequency sound waves as higher-pitched sounds. Lower-frequency sound waves have a lower perceived pitch. In this activity, you will be creating an instrument and using it to explore the properties of sound waves.

MATERIALS

- Piece of paper
- Pair of scissors
- Ruler

PREPARATION

- Use your scissors to cut a 3 by 8 1/2 inch (7.6 by 21.6 cm) rectangle from your paper.

- Fold your rectangle in half lengthwise so that the shorter ends are touching. Make a strong crease.

56

- With your rectangle folded, fold each end back up to the middle crease, in the opposite direction of your original fold. Your paper should have three folds so that it's in the shape of a "W" when viewed from the side.

- Turn your paper around so that your first fold is facing toward you.

- Holding the paper folded, use your scissors to cut a small triangle (1/4 to 1/2 inch [0.6 to 1.3 cm] at the base) at the center of the fold. If you open the paper up, it should look like a small diamond.

PROCEDURE ••••••••••••••••••••••••••••••••••••

- Keeping the paper folded, turn it around so that the cutout is on the side facing away from you.

- Hold the paper horizontally so that it looks a little like a paper mouth.

- Gently press the two lips of the paper mouth to your own lips. Hold it in place by pressing your pointer or middle fingers into the top crease, and your thumbs into the bottom crease.

- Keeping your lips parted, forcefully blow out (don't purse your lips, keep them relaxed).

- If you don't hear a sound right away, try opening your mouth slightly wider, and open your paper mouth slightly wider as well.

- Try slightly different configurations until you get a strong squawk—you'll know it when you hear it!

- Practice your squawking while making observations. *What do you notice about the paper when you're squawking? Does it move? How would you describe the movement?*

- Find the smallest possible gap you can have between the lips of your paper mouth while still getting a sound. Listen to the sound. *What does it sound like?*

- Find the largest possible gap you can have between the lips of your paper mouth while still getting a sound. Listen to the sound. *How does the sound differ when the gap is smaller compared to when it is wider? Does one sound lower or higher than the other?*

ExTRA

Test different-sized triangle cutouts. *How does the size of the cutout affect the sound and performance of your squawker?*

OBSERVATIONS AND RESULTS · · · · · · · ·

In this activity, you created a lot of noise while exploring the physics of sound! You should have observed that as your paper squawked it also vibrated gently in your hand. This tells you something about the sound that you're generating with your squawker. As you blow into it, you cause the paper to vibrate. Those vibrations generate sound waves, and when those sound waves reach our ears we perceive them as a distinct squawking sound.

When you made the gap smaller in your squawker, you should have noticed that the sound became higher pitched. Because you were forcing the same amount of air through a smaller space, you caused the paper to vibrate more quickly. Our ears perceive those faster vibrations as a higher-pitched sound. This is similar to how the thinner strings on a guitar make a higher-pitched sound. They can vibrate faster and therefore produce higher-frequency sound waves.

When you made the gap in your paper squawker larger, you should have noticed that the sound became lower. In this case, you were increasing the space while blowing the same amount of air, and the resulting vibrations of the paper were slower. These slower vibrations create lower-frequency sound waves, which our ears perceive as lower-pitched sounds.

CLEANUP

Recycle the paper. Return the scissors and ruler to the places where you found them.

THE SCIENTIFIC METHOD

The scientific method helps scientists—and students—gather facts to prove whether an idea is true. Using this method, scientists come up with ideas and then test those ideas by observing facts and drawing conclusions. You can use the scientific method to develop and test your own ideas!

Question: What do you want to learn? What problem needs to be solved? Be as specific as possible.

Research: Learn more about your topic and refine your question.

Hypothesis: Form an educated guess about what you think will answer your question. This allows you to make a prediction you can test.

Experiment: Create a test to learn if your hypothesis is correct. Limit the number of variables, or elements of the experiment that could change.

Analysis: Record your observations about the progress and results of your experiment. Then analyze your data to understand what it means.

Conclusion: Review all your data. Did the results of the experiment match the prediction? If so, your hypothesis was correct. If not, your hypothesis may need to be changed.

GLOSSARY

buoyancy: An object's ability to float in water or air.

distance: How far one object is from another object or point.

distill: The process that uses heat to separate a liquid solution.

elastic: A material that returns to its original shape after being stretched.

equilibrium: The state of being balanced.

force: The push or pull of an object that makes it move or stay in place.

frequency: The number of waves that pass a point in a set amount of time.

granular: Something that has a grainy texture.

gravity: A force that brings two objects together.

mass: The amount of matter that makes up an object.

matter: Anything that has weight and takes up space.

particle: The smallest possible unit of matter.

pressure: The force over a specific area.

solution: A mixture of two or more substances.

solvent: A substance that dissolves another substance.

surface tension: A force that causes liquid to act like a sheet.

vacuum: A space with nothing in it.

vortex: A spinning flow of fluid.

ADDITIONAL RESOURCES

Books

Firth, Rachel, Minna Lacey, and Darran Stobbart. *Physics for Beginners.* London, UK: Usborne Publishing Ltd., 2022.

Heinecke, Liz Lee. *Physics for Kids: Science Experiments and Activities Inspired by Awesome Physicists, Past and Present.* Beverly, MA: Quarry, 2022.

Somara, Dr. Shini. *Everyday STEM Science – Physics.* London, UK: Kingfisher, 2022.

Websites

Discovery Education
sciencefaircentral.com

Exploratorium
www.exploratorium.edu/explore/activities

Science Buddies
www.sciencebuddies.org/science-fair-projects/project-ideas/list

Science Fun for Everyone!
www.sciencefun.org/?s=science+fair

Videos

Fun with Physics
https://wqed.pbslearningmedia.org/resource/fun-with-physics-media-gallery/hands-on-science/

Science Friction: Physics
https://wqed.pbslearningmedia.org/resource/d307f985-2610-4ea3-bc19-77d5ee4fa432/science-friction-physics-video-compact-science/

INDEX